I0605097

Love

Love

Essential Literary Themes

by Maggie Combs

Essential Library

An Imprint of Abdo Publishing | abdopublishing.com

abdopublishing.com

Published by Abdo Publishing, a division of ABDO, PO Box 398166, Minneapolis, Minnesota 55439.

Printed in the United States of America, North Mankato, Minnesota
042015
092015

Cover Photo: Shutterstock Images
Interior Photos: RKO Radio Pictures/Photofest, 13; Walt Disney Productions/Photofest, 15; Walt Disney Productions/Album/Newscom, 17; Walt Disney Pictures/Everett Collection, 19, 26; Walt Disney Animation Studios/Newscom, 21, 29; Walt Disney Studios Motion Pictures/Photofest, 23; iStockphoto, 35, 36; Donald Stampfli/AP Images, 39; North Wind Picture Archives, 43, 49; Bettmann/Corbis, 47; Chris Pizzello/Invision/AP Images, 55; Rex Features/AP Images, 57, 58, 65, 67, 73; Jaap Buitendijk/Summit Entertainment/Everett Collection, 60, 75; Penguin Books/Photofest, 81; MGM/Photofest, 83, 89, 91, 96; Mary Evans/Ronald Grant/Everett Collection, 86

Editor: Jenna Gleisner
Series Designer: Maggie Villaume

Library of Congress Control Number: 2015931038
Cataloging-in-Publication Data

Combs, Maggie.
Love / Maggie Combs.
p. cm. -- (Essential literary themes)
Includes bibliographical references and index.
ISBN 978-1-62403-806-8
1. American literature--Themes, motives--Juvenile literature. 2. American literature--History and criticism--Juvenile literature. I. Title.
810--dc23

2015931038

Contents

1

INTRODUCTION TO

Themes in Literature

Do you find yourself drawn to the same types of stories? Are your favorite characters on a quest? Are they seeking revenge? Or are your favorite stories about love? Love, revenge, a quest—these are all examples of themes. Although each story is different, many stories focus on similar themes. You can expand your understanding of the books you read by recognizing the common themes within them.

What Is a Theme?

A theme is a concept or idea that shows up again and again in various works of art, literature, music, theater, film, and other endeavors throughout history. Some themes revolve around a story's plot. For example, a play about a young girl moving away from home and learning the ways of the world would be considered a coming of age story. But themes are not always so easily noticed. For example, a work might have allusions. Allusions are references, sometimes indirect, to other works or historical events. Themes might also relate to specific characters or subjects of a work. For example, many stories present heroes or villains. These common character types are often called archetypes.

How Do You Uncover a Theme?

Themes are presented in different ways in different works, so you may not always be aware of them. Many works have multiple themes. Uncover themes by asking yourself questions about the work. What is the main point or lesson of the story? What is the main conflict? What do the characters want? Where does the story take place? In many cases, themes may not be apparent until after a close study, or analysis, of the text.

What Is an Analysis?

Writing an analysis allows you to explore the themes in a work. In an analysis, you can consider themes in multiple ways. You can describe what themes are present in a work. You can compare one work to another to see how the presentation of a theme differs between the two forms. You can see how the use of a particular theme either supports or rejects society's norms. Rather than attempt to discover the author's purpose in creating a work, an analysis reveals what *you* see in the work.

Raising your awareness of themes through analysis allows you to dive deeper into the work itself. You may begin to see similarities between all creative works that you encounter. You may also improve your own writing by expanding your understanding of how stories use themes to engage readers.

Forming a Thesis

Form your questions about how a theme is presented in a work or multiple works and find answers within the work itself. Then you can create a thesis. The thesis is the key point in your analysis. It is your argument about the work. For example, if you want to argue that the theme of a book is love, your thesis could be worded as follows: Allison Becket's novel *On the Heartless Road* asserts that receiving love is critical to the human experience.

How to Make a Thesis Statement

In an analysis, a thesis statement typically appears at the end of the introductory paragraph. It is usually only one sentence long and states the author's main idea.

Providing Evidence

Once you have formed a thesis, you must provide evidence to support it. Evidence will usually take the form of examples and quotations from the work itself, often including dialogue from a character. You may wish to address what others have written about the work. Quotes from these individuals may help support your claim. If you find any quotes or examples that contradict your thesis, you will need to create an argument against them. For instance: Many critics claim the theme of love is secondary to that of revenge, as the main character, Carly, sabotages the lives of her loved ones throughout the novel. However, the novel's resolution proves that Carly's experience with love is the key to her humanity.

How to Support a Thesis Statement

An analysis should include several arguments that support the thesis's claim. An argument is one or two sentences long and is supported by evidence from the work being discussed. Organize the arguments into paragraphs. These paragraphs make up the body of the analysis.

Concluding the Essay

After you have written several arguments and included evidence to support them, finish the essay with a conclusion. The conclusion restates the ideas from the thesis and summarizes some of the main points from the essay. The conclusion's final thought often considers additional implications for the essay or gives the reader something to ponder further.

How to Conclude an Essay

Begin your conclusion with a recap of the thesis and a brief summary of the most important or strongest arguments. Leave readers with a final thought that puts the essay in a larger context or considers its wider implications.

In This Book

In this book, you will read summaries of works, each followed by an analysis. Critical thinking sections will give you a chance to consider other theses and questions about the work. Did you agree with the author's analysis? What other questions are raised by the thesis and its arguments? You can also see other directions the author could have pursued to analyze the work. Then, in the Analyze It section in the final pages of this book, you will have an opportunity to create your own analysis paper.

Love

The book you are reading focuses on the theme of love and friendship. The theme of love is not always about romance. It can be about love in a family or love between friends. It can even be about loving oneself. Creative works often choose to follow either a society's typical understanding of love or seek to teach the audience a new way of thinking about love. Because the desire for love is often thought to be essential to the human experience, love is a major theme—or at least a supporting undercurrent—of most literature and art.

Look for the Guides

Throughout the chapters that analyze the works, thesis statements have been highlighted. The box next to the thesis helps explain what questions are being raised about the work. Supporting arguments have also been highlighted. The boxes next to the arguments help explain how these points support the thesis. The conclusions are also accompanied by explanatory boxes. Look for these guides throughout each analysis.

2

AN OVERVIEW OF

Disney Fairy Tales

In the Disney film *Snow White and the Seven Dwarfs*, Snow White is a beautiful maiden who must escape the jealousy of her stepmother, the Evil Queen, who wants to kill Snow White for being the fairest in the land. After hearing the Evil Queen plans to have her killed, Snow White flees. With the help of some woodland creatures, Snow White discovers a cottage in the woods, owned by seven dwarfs. The dwarfs take her in and she keeps house for them while they try to protect her from the Evil Queen.

Eventually, the Evil Queen finds where Snow White is hiding. The Evil Queen transforms herself into an old woman with an enchanted apple. Although the

Disney's archetypal princess, exemplified by Snow White, is a damsel in distress who needs saving in the form of love's first kiss.

woodland animals try to get the dwarfs home with enough time to save Snow White, they are too late. Snow White accepts the enchanted apple from the disguised Evil Queen and eats it, falling into an eternal sleep. The dwarfs put Snow White in a glass coffin, where the prince finds her. They had met once before while Snow White was drawing water from the well. The prince bestows on Snow White love's first kiss, which breaks her free from the Evil Queen's spell. Snow White and the prince live happily ever after.

Cinderella

Cinderella is the story of a damsel in distress who is rescued through her friendship with animals and her fairy godmother. After Cinderella's father dies, her wicked stepmother and stepsisters force her to work as a maid in her own home. Her only friends are the mice, birds, and other animals that reside on the estate. She hears about a ball hosted by the king to honor his son and help the prince choose a mate, but her stepsisters destroy her only dress suitable for a ball. Cinderella believes she will not be able to attend the ball, but to her surprise, a fairy godmother comes and transforms her tattered dress into a ball gown with glass slippers and a

Cinderella is a damsel in distress who must serve her wicked stepmother and stepsisters.

pumpkin and mice into a carriage and four horses. She warns Cinderella it will all vanish at midnight.

At the ball, the prince becomes bored with the young maidens being paraded before him. When Cinderella arrives, he immediately falls for her and asks her to dance. They dance until the clock chimes midnight, and Cinderella runs away as the enchantment wears off, accidentally leaving behind a glass slipper. The king sends his messenger throughout the kingdom, searching for the girl whose foot fits the glass slipper, but Cinderella's stepmother locks her away in a tower.

Cinderella's animal friends find the key and release her from the tower just before the messenger leaves. The glass slipper breaks, but Cinderella brings out its mate, proving herself the prince's love. Cinderella and the prince marry and live happily ever after.

Sleeping Beauty

In *Sleeping Beauty*, a king and queen finally have the child they have always longed for. All the country comes to celebrate the baby Princess Aurora, and she is promised to marry young Prince Phillip. Three fairies bring gifts for the princess, but one evil fairy named Maleficent is not invited to the gathering. In her anger, she curses Princess Aurora to die by pricking her finger on a spinning wheel on her sixteenth birthday. The good fairies counter the curse, changing the consequences from death to a sleep from which she can only be awoken by true love's kiss. In an effort to keep Princess Aurora safe, the king orders all spinning wheels to be destroyed, and he allows the good fairies to take the princess away to the woods to live in secret until she turns 16. Princess Aurora meets Prince Phillip in the woods and falls in love with him, neither of them knowing they are already betrothed to each other.

Similar to Snow White, Princess Aurora must also be awakened by true love's first kiss.

On her sixteenth birthday, the fairies bring Princess Aurora home to her family, but she is not as safe as they think. Maleficent lures Princess Aurora into an old chamber with a spinning wheel, where she pricks her finger. The good fairies put the whole land under an enchanted sleep so they can search for her true love. Maleficent has imprisoned Prince Phillip, but when the fairies realize he is Princess Aurora's true love, they free him. Although Maleficent transforms into a giant dragon, Prince Phillip defeats her. He goes to Princess Aurora and awakens her with true love's kiss. They live happily ever after.

Frozen

Frozen centers on the lives of two princess sisters, Elsa and Anna. The oldest sister, Elsa, was born with a powerful gift. She can create ice and snow. One night, her younger sister Anna wakes her to play in the wintry wonderland Elsa has created. However, Elsa does not fully understand how to control her power and accidentally hits Anna with her ice power while they are playing.

The king and queen of Arendelle rush their daughters to the woods to find trolls with healing powers. The grandfather troll removes the ice from Anna's head, along with all memories of Elsa's powers. He advises Elsa's parents to keep Elsa concealed until she learns to control her power. Although he warns them that fear will be her enemy, he does not give any wisdom on how her power can be controlled. Elsa's parents close up the castle, protecting Elsa from curious eyes as she works to understand her power. Despite their best efforts, her power only grows as she stays hidden from the entire world, including her sister Anna.

After their parents tragically die, Anna feels completely alone in the large castle as Elsa remains shut

After accidentally unleashing her ice powers on Arendelle, Elsa builds herself an ice castle in the mountains, isolated from everyone.

in her room. The castle gates are finally opened for Elsa's coronation, letting Anna experience the outside world for the first time. Naïve Anna is swept off her feet by the first man she meets outside of the gates, the dashing Prince Hans of the Southern Isles. At the coronation, Hans proposes marriage and Anna accepts, but when they ask for Queen Elsa's blessing, she refuses to give it. Anna and Elsa argue, and Elsa's anger builds up and explodes in an expression of her ice power.

Elsa flees to the mountains, finally unleashing her full power and creating a beautiful snow and ice palace on top of the highest peak. Anna soon follows her sister, but when her horse runs off, she must enlist the help of a man she meets at a trading post. Kristoff and his reindeer Sven agree to help Anna when she buys the supplies they cannot afford. Along the way, they meet comical Olaf, a living snowman Elsa created, who joins their journey. With Kristoff's begrudging help, Anna finally makes it to Elsa's ice palace. Anna begs her sister to come down and fix the eternal winter that has fallen on Arendelle. Elsa does not know how to control or reverse her power, and when her fears grow stronger she explodes again, accidentally hitting Anna in the heart with her ice power.

Kristoff takes Anna to his adoptive family, the trolls, for healing. The grandfather troll pronounces that because the ice power hit her heart instead of her head this time, only an act of true love can save her. Otherwise, she will turn entirely to ice. One troll suggests a true love's kiss, so Kristoff and Olaf whisk Anna back to Arendelle for a kiss from Hans.

Kristoff and Olaf successfully bring Anna to Hans. But after they leave her, Hans refuses to kiss Anna, explaining that he was only using her to gain the throne of Arendelle. He leaves Anna and goes to battle Elsa

As of 2014, *Frozen* became the highest-grossing animated film of all time.

in an effort to make her thaw the winter. When Elsa explains she cannot control her power, Hans decides to kill her. Across the ice, Olaf desperately tries to help Anna reach Kristoff, whom they realize truly loves her. Anna stumbles toward Kristoff, but when she notices Prince Hans raising his sword against Elsa, she changes course and steps in front of the blade, turning fully into ice as Hans's sword hits her. Anna's act of self-sacrifice and true love unthaws her. Elsa realizes if she stops living in fear and focuses on love, she can unthaw all of Arendelle and gain control of her ice power. Kristoff and Anna finally kiss as the story concludes. They then join Olaf, Sven, and Elsa to ice-skate in the palace courtyard.

3

Frozen's Modern Love

The influence of Disney movies on US society's understanding of love is unquestionable. Many children grow up watching Disney movies, particularly the fairy tales. The fairy tales often serve as a child's first exposure to a love story. One way to understand the power of Disney fairy tales is to recognize their reliance on archetypes. An archetype is something that repeats often in literature, such as a plot or character type, and evokes emotions. Disney's original fairy tale movies *Snow White and the Seven Dwarfs*, *Cinderella*, and *Sleeping Beauty* use three major archetypes to develop their love stories: the dashing prince, the damsel in distress, and the power of true love's kiss. Disney's fairy tale *Frozen* breaks

Through the main character Anna and her actions, *Frozen* defies Disney's usual take on love.

Thesis

A thesis statement is the main argument of an essay. The thesis statement for this essay builds on the sentence before it, stating, "Disney's fairy tale *Frozen* breaks old archetypes to create a modern understanding of love within the fairy tale genre."

Argument One

The first argument states: "The dashing prince serves as the archetype for the main character's love interest in most Disney fairy tales, but *Frozen*'s Kristoff breaks this tradition." This argument requires two paragraphs, one outlining the archetype of the dashing prince in the old fairy tales and a second contrasting it with the love interest in *Frozen*.

old archetypes to create a modern understanding of love within the fairy tale genre.

The dashing prince serves as the archetype for the main character's love interest in most Disney fairy tales, but *Frozen*'s Kristoff breaks this tradition. The archetypal dashing prince is always handsome, but his personality remains undeveloped through the story. Snow White meets her prince at a wishing well when she is working as a maid. The prince is enchanted by her voice and they sing together, but that is the extent of their relationship. In *Cinderella*, the handsome prince is a background character. He has no distinguishing personality traits, never expresses an opinion, and yawns his way through his father's plan to marry him off to an eligible young maiden. He falls in love with Cinderella immediately, but when she goes missing, he does nothing to find her. It is the king's assistant who eventually reunites the couple. In *Sleeping Beauty*, Prince Phillip falls in love with Princess Aurora when he hears her singing in the woods. Prince Phillip is certainly the most admirable of these handsome princes. He stands up for his choice in love rather than blindly following his father's plan for his marriage. He not only kisses Princess Aurora to save her, but he also defeats the evil fairy Maleficent in dragon form using an enchanted sword.

Frozen contrasts these seemingly simple princes with Kristoff, the antiprince. First, Disney distracts the viewer by introducing Prince Hans, a character who fits in well with previous Disney archetypes. He is handsome, wealthy, and rides a horse. But something sinister lurks beneath. Eventually Prince Hans becomes the villain of the story, and the real love interest is revealed: Kristoff. Kristoff is not princely in any way. In fact, an entire song is devoted to his flaws. He admits to picking his boogers and eating them. One reoccurring joke of the movie is that he smells. Kristoff is more

Viewers are at first led to believe Prince Hans will be Anna's love interest and will eventually save the day.

socially comfortable with reindeer and trolls than he is with humans. He is obviously poor, not rich and royally connected. His initial reaction to Princess Anna is annoyance rather than love. Kristoff is the antithesis to the archetype of the handsome prince.

The common archetype for the main princess character of Disney fairy tales is the damsel in distress, yet Princess Anna does not fit this archetype. Snow White is forced to live as a maid. She constantly

Argument Two

The second argument states: "The common archetype for the main princess character of Disney fairy tales is the damsel in distress, yet Princess Anna does not fit this archetype." The second argument also requires two paragraphs, one focusing on the old fairy tales and a second detailing how the archetype is broken in *Frozen*.

needs rescuing, first by woodland creatures and the seven dwarfs, and finally by her prince. *Cinderella* follows a similar plot: Cinderella's stepmother forces her into a life of servitude. The household animals help her with her daily duties and acquire what she needs to attend the ball. When her dress is ruined, Cinderella's fairy godmother steps in to dress her for the ball. When Cinderella's stepmother locks her in her room so she cannot try on the glass slipper, it is the cunningness of the mice and dog that free Cinderella. *Sleeping Beauty*'s Princess Aurora, who faces loneliness instead of labor, is also a damsel in distress. The woodland animals try to fix her problem by arranging a chance meeting between her and Prince Phillip. Even with the help of three fairies, Princess Aurora still manages to fall into Maleficent's spinning wheel trap. She is finally rescued from her enchanted sleep by Prince Phillip. All three of these examples cast female characters as incapable of solving their own problems.

The main character of *Frozen*, Princess Anna, does not fit the damsel in distress archetype. In fact, she is never really in distress. Although she lives a confined life in the castle at the beginning of her story, Anna becomes the master of her own fate when Elsa runs away on coronation day. She chooses, against the advice of Prince Hans, to follow her sister into the mountains. Then, instead of winning Kristoff's help through love, she helps him pay for his supplies to assist her. When Kristoff's sled breaks while helping Anna, she insists on buying him a new one because she is wealthier. If someone tells her she cannot do something, her immediate reaction is to try it. For example, she goes after Elsa, climbs the mountain even after Kristoff tells her it is impossible, beats off the wolves when Kristoff tells her to stay put, and saves Elsa. Although people around Anna may underestimate her, she always has complete confidence in herself. Unlike Cinderella, Princess Aurora, and Snow White, who are constantly relying on the strength of others, Princess Anna resolves her own problems.

Another common Disney archetype *Frozen* does not adhere to is the plot device of true love's kiss. In *Snow White*, love's first kiss has the power to bring Snow White out of the evil sleeping spell the Evil Queen put on her.

Argument Three

The final argument states: "Another common Disney archetype *Frozen* does not adhere to is the plot device of true love's kiss." This paragraph focuses on the love between the sisters instead of between Anna and Kristoff.

Anna takes the lead in pursuing her sister.

In *Sleeping Beauty*, Princess Aurora is also awoken from her enchanted sleep by the power of true love's kiss, which is bestowed on her by Prince Phillip. In *Frozen*, the grandfather troll king tells Anna that only an act of true love can save her. One of the other trolls suggests true love's kiss, harkening back to Disney's archetype. However, Princess Anna never receives such a kiss because Prince Hans does not actually love her and Kristoff cannot get to her in time. Kristoff and Anna do eventually kiss, but there is no magical power to it. Denying the old archetypes, Princess Anna herself performs the act of true love that saves her from a frozen heart. She shows true love when she sacrifices herself to save Elsa. Instead of being a passive recipient of the act of true love, Anna controls her own destiny by saving herself through her love for her sister.

Disney's early fairy tale films *Snow White and the Seven Dwarfs*, *Cinderella*, and *Sleeping Beauty* rely on the archetypes of the handsome prince, damsel in distress, and true love's kiss. In *Frozen*, Disney breaks through these archetypes, offering a new kind of fairy tale. Audiences are happy to accept this new look at love. This new form of fairy tale features an average-guy love interest. And instead of a princess who needs saving, *Frozen* offers a driven and confident princess who controls her own destiny, acting selflessly out of love for her sister. These new archetypes reflect a contemporary understanding of love.

Conclusion

The last paragraph of the critique serves as a conclusion. This paragraph must restate the main arguments of the essay. It also offers one final point to tie the previous arguments together. The final sentence restates the thesis.

Thinking Critically

Now it's your turn to assess the essay. Consider these questions:

1. This essay focuses on Princess Anna as the main character and does not include Queen Elsa. What archetype might Queen Elsa break?
2. One archetype not mentioned in the essay is "happily ever after." Do you enjoy stories that do not end with a happily ever after? Why or why not?
3. Do you think this essay's conclusion supports the thesis? Why or why not?

Other Approaches

Many other archetypes could be used to develop an analysis of love as a theme in *Frozen*. The theme of love can be analyzed outside of archetypes. A feminist critique could lead to an analysis of Anna's experiences with romantic love or an examination of the love between the two sisters.

Love Conquers All

One prevalent archetype in Disney movies is the concept that love conquers all. In *Frozen*, this archetype centers mostly on Elsa. She struggles to control her icy powers. The more afraid Elsa is of her own power, the more out of control it becomes. When Elsa decides to "let it go," she regains some control but still cannot keep Arendelle from experiencing an eternal winter. In her fear, she loses control and injures Anna again. Finally, when Anna's love has the power to thaw her frozen heart, Elsa makes her discovery: love will thaw. As she embraces love, her power turns from something dark and twisted into something joyful. A thesis for this kind of essay might read: The true hero of *Frozen* is not Anna or Elsa, but love itself.

Sisterly Love

Feminist critique often looks at how the relationships between women are portrayed in a work of art. The relationship between Elsa and her sister Anna is complex. A thesis analyzing their relationship from a feminist viewpoint could argue: At first glance, *Frozen* appears to be about the powerful love between sisters, but with deeper study, the story shows Elsa's domineering power and manipulative control over her younger sister Anna.

4

AN OVERVIEW OF

Shakespeare's Sonnets

The sonnet, or "little song," was created in Italy in the 1200s.[1] In the 1300s, Italian poet Petrarch standardized the form. The Petrarchan sonnet is divided into one section of eight lines called an octet or octave, followed by a second section of six lines called a sestet. The octet usually presents a problem or question. The first line of the sestet generally marks the volta, or turn. As the term implies, the volta turns the poem to provide an answer to the problem or question raised in the octet. Petrarch focused his sonnets on one love: Laura. It is unclear whether Laura truly existed or was a symbol of Petrarch's idea of the perfect woman. The use of

Shakespeare is credited with the formation of the Shakespearian sonnet.

Petrarch made the sonnet poem form popular in Italy.

Petrarch's sonnet did not become widespread in Europe and England until the Renaissance of the 1500s.

In the hands of the capable English Renaissance poets, namely William Shakespeare, the sonnet took on a slightly new shape. Instead of being divided into an octet and sestet, it was divided into three groups of four lines, called quatrains, and a final set of two lines, called a couplet. This new grouping allowed for three sections of exposition with a final summary in the couplet in contrast to the problem-answer form of the Petrarchan sonnet. This new format may have led to the sonnet's incredible popularity in England. More than 1,200 sonnets still exist in print from the 1590s.[2] Many poets wrote sonnets that were meant to be read as a group called a sequence. Such sonnet sequences were usually addressed to the speaker's beloved, in the tradition of Petrarch's Laura.

Understanding Sonnets

Sonnets are generally composed of 14 lines following a specific format. Although line divisions can differ among poets, Shakespeare always used three quatrains and a couplet. The Shakespearean sonnet follows the rhyme scheme *abab cdcd efef gg*, each letter representing a repeated or new rhyming word. Meter considers the number of syllables in each line and the rhythm of stressed syllables. Iambic pentameter is employed in Shakespearean sonnets, which means there are ten syllables in each line following a rhythm of unstressed-stressed syllables.

It is this defined format that lends a sonnet its strength. The divisions of the lines allows the poet to link separate images to each other. If the standard meter is broken, the reader must immediately take note of the importance of that word. The final couplet often offers an unexpected conclusion to the sonnet's theme. To discover the meaning of a sonnet, a reader must follow the speaker's train of thought while noting when the speaker breaks the traditional form of the sonnet for specific emphasis. Noting the turn and focusing on the final couplet helps the reader discover the meaning of the sonnet.

Shakespeare's Sonnets

In 1609, Thomas Thorpe published 154 of Shakespeare's sonnets, along with a long poem titled *A Lover's Complaint*, which does not follow a sonnet format. Although the sonnets were published after the sonnet trend of the 1590s, it is unclear exactly when in Shakespeare's life they were written. There is evidence at least some of the sonnets were written and, although not published as a sequence, were circulating during the 1590s.

Shakespeare's sonnets differ from the majority of sonnets written in his day in their dedication and voice. Sonnets 1 through 126 are dedicated to a young man, whom scholars believe was a friend, instead of the conventional female beloved. Sonnets 127 through 152 focus on a female love called the "dark lady." The

The last two sonnets published in Thorpe's collection focus on Cupid, the mythological god of love.

final two sonnets are about the mythological god of love, Cupid. Although many try to identify "the friend" and the "dark lady," it is impossible to know whether the sonnets were written about Shakespeare's real life. The speaker's voice in the sonnets is certainly more complicated than the stereotypically smitten lover of Shakespeare's day. It is sometimes adoring but often cynical. It can be proud or insecure. It is obsessed with romance or only interested in physical love, but above all else, the speaker is richly in love. It is this authentic love that still resonates with readers today.

Sonnet 18

SHALL I compare thee to a summer's day?
Thou art more lovely and more temperate:
Rough winds do shake the darling buds of May,
And summer's lease hath all too short a date:

Sometime too hot the eye of heaven shines,
And often is his gold complexion dimm'd:
And every fair from fair sometime declines,
By chance, or nature's changing course,
untrimm'd.

But thy eternal summer shall not fade
Nor lose possession of that fair thou ow'st;
Nor shall Death brag thou wander'st in his shade,
When in eternal lines to time thou grow'st: —

So long as men can breathe, or eyes can see,
So long lives this, and this gives life to thee.[3]

Sonnet 130

MY mistress' eyes are nothing like the sun;
Coral is far more red than her lips' red;
If snow be white, why then her breasts are dun;
If hairs be wires, black wires grow on her head.

I have seen roses damask'd, red and white,
But no such roses see I in her cheeks;
And in some perfumes is there more delight
Than in the breath that from my mistress reeks.

I love to hear her speak, yet well I know
That music hath a far more pleasing sound;
I grant I never saw a goddess go;
My mistress, when she walks, treads on the ground:

And yet, by heaven, I think my love as rare
As any she belied with false compare.[4]

5

Shakespeare's Contrasting Techniques

Although a part of the sonnet trend of the 1590s, Shakespeare's sonnets are anything but conventional. Shakespeare did not blindly follow the accepted love conventions of his time. Instead, he boldly explored new concepts using literary techniques as tools to convey his meaning.

Ideas of love in the sonnets of Elizabethan England were still heavily influenced by courtly love conventions and their Petrarchan predecessors. Courtly love is characterized by an intense physical reaction to falling in love. The lover becomes sick with love: sighing, weeping, fainting, losing sleep and appetite, and losing

The concept of love in most Elizabethan sonnets grew out of the courtly love conventions of the Middle Ages.

interest in other parts of life. The three main principles are devotion to an idealized form of womanhood, loyalty to the beloved, and worshiping adoration of the beloved. Courtly love conventions reached their heights in England during the medieval period, but they continued influencing English literature until the 1800s. According to Lillian Herlands Hornstein, author of *The Readers Companion to World Literature*, Petrarchan sonnets rely on "exaggerated comparisons expressing the beauty, cruelty, and charm of the beloved and the suffering of the forlorn lover."[1] Many of the sonnet writers in the English Renaissance wrote in Petrarchan style, but Shakespeare instead chose to demolish it through literary techniques.

Shakespeare's sonnets break these conventions and usher the theme of love in literature into a new Renaissance understanding. Sonnet 18 contrasts love conventions through hyperbole whereas Sonnet 130 uses satire.

Shakespeare's Sonnet 18

Thesis

The thesis statement claims: "Shakespeare's Sonnet 18 and Sonnet 130 use these contrasting literary techniques to expand the popular understanding of love in Elizabethan England." This essay will focus on the literary techniques Shakespeare used in his Sonnet 18 and Sonnet 130 to defy his contemporary themes of love.

and Sonnet 130 use these contrasting literary techniques to expand the popular understanding of love in Elizabethan England.

Shakespeare uses hyperbole in Sonnet 18 to make a contrast with his society's typical understanding of love. Hyperbole is a literary technique that in its simplest form is an exaggeration. The first line of the poem begins, "Shall I compare thee to a summer's day?" Based on the conventional understanding of analyzing love, the answer should be yes. Instead, Shakespeare uses hyperbole, calling his friend "more lovely" and "more temperate." Shakespeare goes on to explain the problems with being compared to summer. In lines 2 through 4, he asserts summer is too changing and short. The second quatrain continues this idea. The "eye of heaven," or sun, shines sometimes too brightly and other times too little. Altogether, nature changes too much to be a good comparison for his beloved.

The third quatrain marks the turn with its first word, *but*. Now the speaker no longer describes

Argument One

The first argument states: "Shakespeare uses hyperbole in Sonnet 18 to make a contrast with his society's typical understanding of love." This argument begins the analysis of the sonnets in comparison to typical love conventions.

summer, beginning to talk about his beloved. Here he again uses hyperbole. In lines 9 and 10, the beloved is not only like summer, but like an eternal, unfading summer that never loses its beauty. In lines 11 and 12, the speaker finally gets to his point: the eternal words of this poem will make the beloved immortal. The final couplet reiterates this concept: as long as the poem is read, the beloved will be eternal. The immortality of his poem is Shakespeare's final hyperbole that breaks conventional love.

Argument Two

The second argument states: "Shakespeare's Sonnet 130 defies conventional themes of love through the use of satire." An analysis of Sonnet 130 demonstrates how Shakespeare uses humor and satire to change how love is understood.

Shakespeare's Sonnet 130 defies conventional themes of love through the use of satire. Satire is a literary technique that combines criticism and humor to create change. All three quatrains of Sonnet 130 note a specific Petrarchan conceit, and then they deny his love embodies it. Shakespeare's recurring "dark lady" takes her nickname from her description in this sonnet. The woman Shakespeare describes is not beautiful and virtuous. Instead, she has unique features and even

The woman depicted in Sonnet 130 is strikingly opposite from Petrarch's beloved and beautiful Laura.

her own sensuality. Whereas Petrarch's Laura stood as an example to which most Elizabethan sonneteers aspired, Shakespeare creates a love most would not have admired at the time. Shakespeare's "dark lady" does not have shining eyes (line 1), coral lips (line 2), white skin (line 3), or golden hair (line 4). She has neither rosy red or pure white cheeks (lines 5–6) nor lovely smelling

Argument Three

Argument three states: "Although these anti-Petrarchan descriptions may seem cruel yet funny, they seek to reshape the idealized woman of courtly love conventions." This argument will evaluate some of the ways Shakespeare's poetry changed people's perceptions of what a woman of courtly love was.

breath (lines 7–8). Although Shakespeare enjoys when she talks, her voice does not rival the sound of music (lines 9–10). Finally, there is no comparing her to a goddess (lines 11–12).

Although these anti-Petrarchan descriptions may seem cruel yet funny, they seek to reshape the idealized woman of courtly love conventions. Shakespeare's final couplet shows his true intent: despite her unorthodox traits, the speaker loves her just as deeply, or more so, than writers who use false comparisons to describe their loves. The "dark lady" is not only a combination of poetic tradition, but a unique individual worthy of his love. Sonnet 130's satirical take on the beloved is a strong commendation of traditional love conventions, celebrating individual beauty.

Shakespeare could not blindly recommend the kind of love common to the literature of his time. Instead of following the courtly love conventions still prevalent from the medieval time period or reusing the

SHAKE-SPEARES

SONNETS.

Neuer before Imprinted.

AT LONDON
By *G. Eld* for *T. T.* and are
to be solde by *Iohn Wright*, dwelling
at Christ Church gate.
1609.

Many of Shakespeare's sonnets defy popular conventions.

Conclusion

The last paragraph of the critique serves as a conclusion. Every sentence reviews one of the main points of the essay, relating each point back to the thesis. The thesis is restated in the final sentence of the paragraph.

kind of love popularized by Petrarch's sonnets, Shakespeare blazed a new path to love. Sonnet 18 uses hyperbole to claim love is only eternal through the power of poetry. Sonnet 130 satirizes Petrarch's Laura to create a more realistic woman who is an individual deserving of love. These sonnets are examples of how Shakespeare's larger sonnet sequence developed a new understanding of love among his readers.

Thinking Critically

Now it's your turn to assess the essay. Consider these questions:

1. This essay addresses the theme of love and conventions of Elizabethan England. What other themes do you find in Shakespeare's sonnets?
2. This essay provides three arguments to support its thesis. What is another argument that could be made about Shakespeare's use of literary techniques in Sonnet 18 and Sonnet 130?
3. Some critics argue Sonnet 130 is only meant for humor. Do you agree with the author's assertion that the satire used in Sonnet 130 is meant to show a more realistic love instead of only humor? Why or why not?

Other Approaches

Other attempts to analyze these sonnets from different perspectives will yield different results. An essay solely on Sonnet 18 could focus on how the theme of time works with the theme of love to create a love that transcends time. Sonnet 130 could be considered from a feminist perspective to analyze how Shakespeare asserts his control over his female beloved.

Timeless Love

One of Shakespeare's most prominent themes in his sonnets is time. In many, lengths of time grow throughout the poem. For example, in the first quatrain, time is at its shortest; therefore, the comparison to his love may not be effective. But by the third quatrain, the focus is often on the afterlife and time eternal. A thesis focusing on the relationship between the two themes of time and love in the Sonnet 18 might read: Shakespeare uses the language of time to establish an eternal love.

An Unusual Beloved under Control

A feminist criticism of Sonnet 130 might consider how Shakespeare demeans his unusual mistress to keep her under his control. The final couplet asserts that it is rare for a man to love an ugly woman, which gives the dark lady a final reminder that if she leaves him she is not likely to be loved by another man. The thesis for a feminist criticism of Sonnet 130 might read: Shakespeare verbally abuses his love throughout Sonnet 130 in order to remind her that she would not receive the love of other men.

6

AN OVERVIEW OF *Divergent*

In Veronica Roth's 2011 novel, *Divergent*, Beatrice Prior is a 16-year-old girl growing up in post-apocalyptic Chicago, Illinois. The people in Beatrice's world divide themselves into five factions. Each faction chooses to elevate one character trait above all others, causing divisions that make it difficult for the factions to coexist. Beatrice belongs to the faction Abnegation, which believes in finding fulfillment through selflessness. The faction Amity seeks peace above all. Candor values the truth, without regard to the consequences. Erudite is on a quest for knowledge. None of these factions intrigue Beatrice the way Dauntless does, where people must be brave above all else.

In their final year at school, all students undergo an aptitude test to help—but not determine—their

Roth has become famous for authoring the popular Divergent trilogy.

choice of faction. Beatrice refuses to follow the test's protocols, creating an inconclusive result. Her test giver manually enters a result and warns Beatrice not to tell anyone because her response to the aptitude test marks her as Divergent. Beatrice does not know what Divergent means, but it confirms her fear that she is different in a bad way. Although her father is a leader of Abnegation, Beatrice feels as though she has never really fit in as a member. She makes the unusual decision to switch factions on choosing day. Once Beatrice chooses Dauntless, she must pass an initiation process to become a member.

Dauntless Initiation

When the Dauntless initiates reach the faction's headquarters, Beatrice steps forward to be the first to jump off of the building into the dark pit below to enter the Dauntless compound. In that moment, she begins her transformation into her Dauntless self—Tris. Her bravery earns her some notoriety, and she quickly makes friends with Christina and Al, who are transfers from Candor, and Will, a transfer from Erudite.

Dauntless initiation is physically and emotionally brutal. First, initiates train in combat. Only the top ten

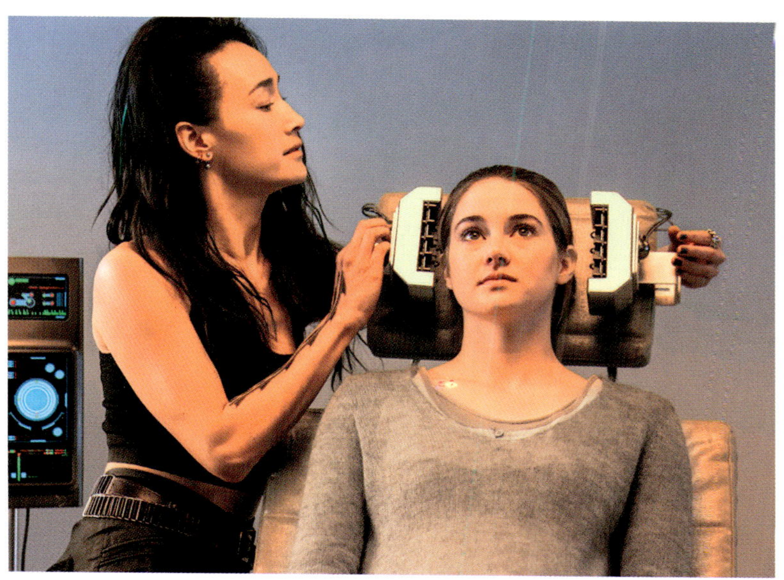

Beatrice's aptitude test marks her as Divergent.

initiates, including both transfers and Dauntless-born, will survive to become Dauntless members. The rest will become factionless, a fate Tris considers worse than death because the factionless live as homeless beggars.

The transfer initiates are taught by Four and Eric, two 18-year-olds only a couple years out of initiation themselves. Eric is a Dauntless leader-in-training who believes "a brave man never surrenders."[1] Four was the Dauntless leaders' first pick to be leader in training, but he constantly avoids their requests despite his natural leadership qualities. Four holds to old Dauntless views and values, insisting "a brave man acknowledges the strength of others."[2] Throughout Tris's initiation, the

Tris trains in combat as part of her initiation into Dauntless.

two instructors constantly disagree on the methods and values they are trying to impart to the incoming initiates. Although Tris is small and unskilled in combat, she is able to increase her ranking by using her intelligence in war games and carefully following Four's wise suggestions. Four seems fascinated by Tris's handling of initiation despite her apparent disadvantages. Tris admires Four and struggles to control her infatuation with a man she considers too old for her and a little dangerous.

Under Eric's direction, Dauntless initiation becomes so brutal that some initiates drop out before reaching the end of the first section. Others, such as Tris's friend Al, become emotionally incapacitated by it. Eric will not tolerate any sign of weakness. When Tris's friend Christina tries to surrender in a fight, he makes her hang from a railing above the deep chasm in the center of the Dauntless compound. Tris wants to help her friend but is afraid Eric will force her to hang above the chasm as well. Tris asks herself, "What's worse: to be idle while someone dies, or to be exiled and empty-handed?"[3] Tris has finally altogether rejected the Abnegation's focus on putting others needs before one's own, so she waits until Eric allows her to assist her friend back to safety.

When the initiates are learning the skill of knife throwing, Eric again chooses one of Tris's friends to serve as a lesson to the others. When timid Al cannot manage to hit the mark, Eric calls for him to retrieve his knives as the other initiates are still throwing. Al refuses, and Eric accuses him of cowardice. In a drastic power play, Eric forces Al to stand against the wall while Four throws knives at him. Tris is not willing to sit and watch Eric put her friend in danger this time. Her selfless side comes out as she speaks up in defense:

Although Tris is angered that Four purposefully injured her with his knife, it only serves to fuel her growing fascination with him.

"Any idiot can stand in front of a target. . . . It doesn't prove anything except that you're bullying us. Which, as I recall, is a sign of cowardice."[4] Eric then forces Tris to take Al's place as Four throws the knives. Tris trusts Four's abilities enough not to flinch as he throws three knives, each closer to her face until the last scrapes the side of her ear as it hits the wall.

Tris finishes stage one just high enough in the ranking not to become factionless. Before the next stage of initiation, Tris's mother visits and warns Tris that if she is Divergent, she must be careful not to stand out in initiation. Tris is surprised by her mother's knowledge of Dauntless initiation and the compound, and she starts to wonder about her mother's background, realizing she has always assumed her mother was originally from Abnegation.

The second stage of initiation immerses the initiates in their deepest fears to help them break free from fear altogether. Each initiate enters a fear simulation similar to the aptitude test. As Four administers Tris's simulations, he quickly recognizes she is Divergent because she is aware in the simulation that it is not real and manipulates the simulation to make it end quickly. Four confronts Tris about her unusual reaction to the simulation and warns Tris to be careful. This only confuses Tris further. She wonders what is wrong in her brain to make her different and labeled as Divergent. She cannot figure out how she became Divergent or what Divergent truly means. Tris finally lets her guard down, trusting Four with the secret of her Divergence, but he is unable to explain to her what Divergence is or why it causes her to respond differently to simulations.

Because of her Divergence, Tris ranks first among the transfer initiates at the end of stage two. Upset by her success, three initiates kidnap her that night and hold her above the chasm, threatening sexual assault and death. Although Tris cannot see her attackers, she recognizes the smell of her close friend Al. Four appears and beats the three attackers, then takes Tris back to his room for safety. Tris finally admits to herself that she is attracted to Four: "He is not sweet or gentle or particularly kind. But he is smart and brave, and even though he saved me, he treated me like I was strong. That is all I need to know."[5]

Al asks for Tris's forgiveness the next day, but Tris refuses. That night Al commits suicide by throwing himself into the chasm. Although Tris knows Al had been slipping emotionally since he started initiation, she cannot help but feel his death is her fault because of her refusal to forgive.

Final Stages of Initiation

The final stage of initiation is the fear landscape: a compilation of all the fears faced in the second stage put into a timed test. To prepare, Four takes Tris through his fear landscape, where she finally learns that his nickname is Four because he only has four fears when most initiates have at least ten. Tris also learns that

Four's real name is Tobias, and he is the abused son of a leader of Abnegation. Tobias finally declares his mutual attraction to Tris, and they share a kiss on the rocks near the chasm. A few days later, Tris completes her fear landscape in front of the Dauntless leaders, achieving the fastest time of all the initiates because she only has seven fears. Tris's final and worst fear is that she will be responsible for the death of her family. Before the fear simulation ends, she is given a gun and told to shoot her family, but she refuses, shooting herself in the head instead. At the end of her fear landscape, she is injected with a tracking device. She spends the afternoon talking to and kissing Tobias in his room before they attend the initiation ceremony separately. Tris finishes first in her class of initiates, even before the Dauntless-born.

Dauntless Army

That night, Tris wakes up to her fellow initiates getting dressed and leaving their dorm in a zombie-like trance. Tris guesses the Erudite faction is controlling the Dauntless through the trackers injected earlier that day. With a mind-controlled Dauntless army, the Erudite will murder Abnegation and seize control of the government. Tris finds Tobias and is relieved that he is also not controlled by his tracker. They make a run for it, but when Tris is shot, Tobias refuses to leave her. They are captured and taken to the leader of Erudite, who injects Tobias with a different kind of serum to control him, one that creates a simulation in his brain to make all friends appear as enemies. Tris is taken to a tank of water to drown, which is one of her fears. Right before she is about to die, her mother breaks the glass and rescues her, revealing her Dauntless upbringing. Together they run through the city streets, searching for the safe house where Tris's father and brother are waiting for them. A group of mind-controlled Dauntless discover them, and Tris's mother is shot while distracting the soldiers, allowing Tris to escape.

At the safe house, Tris meets up with members of the Abnegation leadership, including her own father and brother as well as Tobias's abusive father. They go to Dauntless headquarters, where Tris suspects they will find the computer program controlling the Dauntless army. As Tris attempts to get to the control room, her father is shot and killed. Tris arrives at the control room to find a mind-controlled Tobias, who immediately tries to kill her. She tries to speak to him and help him realize who she is, but nothing works until she allows

Tris and Tobias band together to defeat the Dauntless simulation at the end of the film.

him to almost kill her. When she sacrifices her life because she cannot kill him, he finally hears her through the simulation and breaks free of the mind control. Together, they shut down the Dauntless simulation before leaving on a train with Tobias's father and Tris's brother, escaping to the peaceful faction of Amity. Tobias tells Tris he loves her and they kiss just before the story ends.

7

Tris's Self-Love

Although a story may focus on a romantic relationship between two characters, it does not mean that type of love is the main theme of the story. In *Divergent*, it is not Tris's relationship with Tobias that shapes Tris and her decisions. Instead, it is her relationship with herself that experiences the most growth.

When the story begins, Tris views her differences from society as negative. Through her respect for her new friends and her new understanding of her mother, Tris begins accepting and appreciating her mysterious divergence. Tris grows from a girl who is afraid to love herself into a woman who can defeat the enemy by embracing her differences. In the post-apocalyptic world of *Divergent*, personal value is based on conforming to a faction's chosen characteristic, and it is only when

Through challenges and growing personal acceptance, Tris learns to love herself.

Thesis

The thesis statement reads: "In the post-apocalyptic world of *Divergent*, personal value is based on conforming to a faction's chosen characteristic, and it is only when Tris learns to love all parts of herself and embrace her Divergence that she is able to defeat her enemy." This essay will focus on how forming relationships with others can affect self-perception.

Argument One

The first argument demonstrates why Tris originally feels shame about her personality: "Tris initially feels shame and guilt because she is unable to conform to her original faction, has an inconclusive aptitude test, and cannot eradicate the Abnegation parts of herself after she becomes a member of Dauntless." This argument is necessary to show how Tris changes throughout the novel by establishing her initial behavior.

Tris learns to love all parts of herself and embrace her Divergence that she is able to defeat her enemy.

Tris initially feels shame and guilt because she is unable to conform to her original faction, has an inconclusive aptitude test, and cannot eradicate the Abnegation parts of herself after she becomes a member of Dauntless. Much of Tris's thoughts at the beginning of the story are about her failure to fit in with her own faction. Even these thoughts show her inability to conform to her society because her faction, Abnegation, believes self-focus is wrong. It is so normal for her to see her brother's disapproval of her selfishness that she has his facial expression memorized. She finds her brother's "natural goodness" and "inborn selflessness"irritating.[1] Tris labels her curiosity as a "mistake" and a "betrayal."[2] She believes failing to choose Abnegation is forsaking her family. Although she spends her life trying to be like those around her, Tris finds herself unable to be selfless and truly be part of Abnegation. Finally, she chooses to join Dauntless, telling herself, "I am selfish. I am brave."[3] She changes factions in a desperate attempt to find a place where she does not have to feel shame and guilt for who she is. She denies the selfless part of her personality to embrace her bravery.

When Tris takes the aptitude test, she begins to learn the extent of her differences from her peers. The aptitude test requires her to make a choice that would indicate one faction over another, but Tris refuses. As a result, Tris's test is inconclusive because she shows equal aptitude for Abnegation, Dauntless, and Erudite, marking her as Divergent. Tris's test giver warns her that being Divergent is dangerous and must remain a secret. This result and her test giver's reaction to it only add to Tris's confusion. She does not know what being Divergent really means, why it must be a secret, or why it is dangerous. Tris thinks that if she can only understand what it means to be Divergent, she can understand herself.

After changing factions, Tris believes she must eradicate everything about her old self to become a new person. Every time she finds herself acting or thinking selflessly, she stops her behavior immediately: "It will be difficult to break the habits of thinking Abnegation instilled in me, like tugging a single thread from a complex work of embroidery. But I will find new habits, new thoughts, new rules. I will become something else."[4] She still thinks of her parents' disapproval of her new faction family, particularly the way they dress and the violence they teach, but she tries to reject her need for their approval. Tris's thoughts are no longer about her failure to fit in with the selfless qualities of the Abnegation. She now has the opposite problem: she must control the selfless thoughts she once believed she lacked. Eric warns the initiates attachment to their families and old factions is "shameful."[5] Even by becoming Dauntless, Tris is unable to escape the shame of not truly fitting in with her faction.

Through the initiation process, Tris meets other people who embrace both their old faction's characteristic and Dauntless values, which allows her to start accepting and loving herself. Tris views Dauntless as a place where she can begin again. Her first friends at Dauntless are other transfer initiates, Will from Erudite and Cristina and Al from Candor. Although they all have an aptitude for Dauntless, the factions they grew up in have clearly influenced how they think and react to the world. Will tries to become Dauntless, but he still searches for and values knowledge like an Erudite. Following the ways of their old faction, Candor, both Cristina and Al get in trouble with Dauntless leadership for speaking what they believe rather than blindly following what Dauntless wants them to think. When Christina is selfless toward Tris, Tris begins to recognize everyone has some of each faction in them, even if they are not Divergent. After Al's betrayal and suicide, Tris must rely on the selflessness of her friends to protect her from her enemies in Dauntless. This

Argument Two

The second argument states: "Through the initiation process, Tris meets other people who embrace both their old faction's characteristic and Dauntless values, which allows her to start accepting and loving herself." This argument shows how Tris has to rethink her original self-assessment based on what she respects in her friends.

inspires Tris to get a tattoo of the Abnegation symbol in addition to her Dauntless tattoo, recognizing selflessness as a legitimate part of her personality in addition to her bravery.

Argument Three

The third argument is devoted to Tris's relationship with Tobias and how it has helped her love who she is: "As Tris's respect for Tobias grows into love, she begins to reshape her thinking according to his wisdom as a fellow Abnegation to Dauntless transfer."

As Tris's respect for Tobias grows into love, she begins to reshape her thinking according to his wisdom as a fellow Abnegation to Dauntless transfer. Tobias views Tris's Abnegation background as a strength: "You're from Abnegation," he says, "and it's when you're acting selflessly that you are at your bravest."[6] When Tris feels guilty, Tobias reminds her of the Abnegation concept that guilt should serve as a motivation to do better next time. According to Tobias, "selflessness and bravery aren't all that different. All your life you've been training to forget yourself, so when you're in danger, it becomes your first instinct."[7] Tris does not believe his idea applies to her until Tobias reminds her that she stood in front of throwing knives for her friend. Tobias's view of Tris as both selfless and

After forming a close relationship, Tobias helps Tris learn to love herself.

brave helps Tris transform from a girl who feels ashamed of her personality into a woman who fully accepts herself as a complex and multifaceted person.

After Tris realizes her mother's past, she begins accepting and nurturing the selfless part of her that came from Abnegation rather than loathing it. When Tris's mother comes to Dauntless headquarters on visiting day, Tris learns her mother was once a member of Dauntless

Argument Four

The fourth argument focuses on how Tris's perception of her mother changes and shifts how Tris views herself: "After Tris realizes her mother's past, she begins accepting and nurturing the selfless part of her that came from Abnegation rather than loathing it."

but chose to become Abnegation. Tris wonders, "If my mother was Dauntless, why did she choose Abnegation? Did she love its peace, its routine, its goodness—all the things I miss, when I let myself think about it?"[8] For the first time, Tris is able to see her mother as both selfless and brave. This shift is demonstrated when Tris cleans up an initiate's blood after he is stabbed in the eye. Tris recognizes, "Scrubbing the floor when no one else wanted to was something that my mother would have done. If I can't be with her, the least I can do is act like her sometimes."[9] As Tris goes forward, she starts consulting the wisdom of her mother and Tobias as she makes decisions.

Only when Tris accepts and loves all parts of her personality is she able to stop Erudite's plan to take over the world through mind control. Tris must be brave and selfless to defeat her enemy. When Dauntless is under mind control and Tobias and Tris are pretending to be controlled as well, Tobias tells her they should run,

Argument Five

The fifth argument states: "Only when Tris accepts and loves all parts of her personality is she able to stop Erudite's plan to take over the world through mind control." This argument shows the importance of the change in Tris from shame to acceptance.

Tris begins to love and appreciate her mother in a different way after realizing she was once also Dauntless.

but Tris refuses because she wants to save her family more than she wants to save herself. As Eric puts a gun to Tobias's head, Tris raises her gun even though it will show her enemy she is Divergent and not under control of the serum. Finally, Tris subjects herself to being killed by Tobias rather than have to kill him. It is an act of true acceptance of both parts of herself, the brave and the selfless. She finally recognizes the power she has in being fully herself. This act of brave selflessness helps Tobias break free of his simulation, and together they disarm the program controlling the minds of the Dauntless soldiers. If Tris had not grown to love both the brave and selfless parts of her personality, she would have been unable to defeat the enemy.

Tris's post-apocalyptic world has labeled anyone who does not neatly fit into the factions' categories as Divergent. The leaders believe divergence is bad and should be eradicated to maintain their society. However, after growing through her relationships with others, Tris learns to love all parts of herself: the selfless and the brave. She finally believes her divergence is a good quality despite what her society says. The final sentences of the novel show her acceptance of herself and how her love for herself will now help her become an even stronger person: "I am no longer Tris, the selfless, or Tris, the brave. I suppose that now, I must become more than either."[10] Tris becomes a woman who can defeat her enemy, rather than live in fear of her society.

Conclusion

The last paragraph of the essay serves as a conclusion. It summarizes the main ideas and restates the thesis. This conclusion also goes further, including final evidence that Tris has completely accepted herself by the end of the novel.

Thinking Critically

Now it's your turn to assess the essay. Consider these questions:

1. The thesis statement assumes self-acceptance is the same as self-love. Do you agree or disagree? Why or why not?
2. The author provides five arguments. Can you think of another argument to support the essay's thesis?
3. The conclusion summarizes the essay's thesis and arguments. How could it be reworded or enhanced?

Other Approaches

Self-love is not the only way to understand what *Divergent* says about the theme of love. Other approaches could look at the love between Tris and Tobias. Another analysis might look at how the theme of sacrificial love was influenced by Veronica Roth's religious background.

Religiously Influenced

In *Divergent*, Tris's growth as a character depends on her ability to change from self-centered dismissal of others to laying down her life to save Tobias. Tris initially will not sacrifice for Christina when she is in trouble with Eric but later chooses to stand up for Al when Eric puts him in danger. A thesis based on the actions of Tris's character might read: Veronica Roth's Christian understanding of love as self-sacrifice becomes the theme of love in *Divergent*.

Romance above Reason

An essay focusing on the romantic love between Tris and Tobias could argue Tris falls in love with Tobias impulsively and without thinking. Tris herself often admits she is distracted from initiation and the war brewing in her world by the mere presence of Tobias. A thesis about Tris's love for Tobias could read: Tris's love for Tobias is founded on an unhealthy infatuation with her older instructor.

8

AN OVERVIEW OF *Of Mice and Men*

John Steinbeck's short novel *Of Mice and Men* was published in 1937. He described it as "neither a novel nor a play but . . . a kind of playable novel."[1] In fact, it was adapted for the stage with a production opening on May 21, 1937, and it ran for two months in San Francisco, California, before being adapted for Broadway. *Of Mice and Men* opened on Broadway on November 23, 1937, running for 207 performances, winning awards, and making Steinbeck and his short novel a household name.[2]

Steinbeck intended *Of Mice and Men* to be a new kind of genre, a combination of a play and a novel.

A New Beginning

Of Mice and Men is a tragic story of two migrant ranch workers in California in the 1930s. George is a small and intelligent man with "restless eyes and sharp, strong features."[3] His companion is Lennie, a large man with a mental impairment, who is "shapeless of face with large, pale eyes."[4] George is clearly the leader, constantly yelling at Lennie and instructing him on how he should do everything, even controlling how Lennie drinks his water and when he is allowed to speak.

As the story begins, George and Lennie stop at a clearing by a small pond. They had hopped a bus to their next work assignment, but the bus driver refused to leave them by the ranch. Instead of finishing the long walk, they spend the night by the pond. During their discussion, George notices Lennie is touching something in his pocket. When George demands to see it, Lennie produces a dead mouse, but he swears he did not kill it. Lennie claims he found it dead and kept it in his pocket to touch its soft fur. George becomes angry and tells Lennie to get rid of the mouse. Later that night, George realizes Lennie once again has the mouse. Lennie explains that he loves to pet mice, but when they bite his

Lennie relies completely on George, *above*, for guidance to navigate the confusing world around him.

fingers, he pinches their heads and they die because they are so little.

George becomes angry because it reminds him too much of the reason they had to leave their last farm job. Lennie saw a little girl in a pretty dress and wanted to feel the softness of the fabric. Lennie grabbed the little girl's dress, and even though she screamed, Lennie clamped his hand down and would not let go. The people of the town looked for them, but Lennie and

George were able to sneak away. Now as they plan to start a new job the next morning, George does his best to prepare Lennie not to tell anyone what happened at their last job and not to do something to get them in trouble again.

Before they go to sleep, Lennie begs George to tell him about the farm again. The farm is their dream, their greatest hope for the future. They cling to this dream through the retelling of an idyllic vision in which they are landowners who work for themselves, doing exactly as they please. In the vision, Lennie tends to the bunnies, and together, he and George take care of a cow, a pig, some chickens, and a small garden. Just before they go to bed, George tells Lennie that if they have another problem like at the last ranch, they will meet back at the clearing.

Back at the Ranch

When George and Lennie arrive at the ranch, they enter the bunkhouse and meet the boss and a fellow worker named Candy. The boss is skeptical of Lennie's quiet demeanor, but George is able to talk him into giving both of them a chance. They wait in the bunkhouse until the other workers come back for lunch. As they wait, they meet the boss's son, a hothead named Curley. He gets angry when George does not let Lennie respond to him and starts yelling at Lennie. Candy explains to them, "Curley's like a lot of little guys. He hates big guys. He's alla time picking scraps with big guys."[5] Candy warns George and Lennie that Curley has been angrier since he got married two weeks ago. His wife has been flirting with the other men on the ranch, and Curley is constantly trying to keep an eye on her. George tells Lennie to stay away from Curley and his wife as much as he can because he does not want Curley to find a reason to fight Lennie.

That evening, the foreman, Slim, gives a puppy to Lennie. Lennie is obsessed with the puppy and does not want to come in from the barn even to sleep. The foreman is surprised George and Lennie travel together, but George explains that Lennie's aunt made George promise to take care of him. Later, Candy comes in with his old dog. All the workers pester him to put down his old stinky dog, and after much protest, Candy gives in. He cannot bring himself to shoot the dog, so another worker does it for him. Later, Candy regrets that he let someone else shoot his dog. He wishes he had done it himself.

Throughout the novel and film, Lennie finds comfort in soft things, such as his puppy.

Shared Dreams

Eventually all the workers leave the bunkhouse except George, Lennie, and Candy, who is lying quietly in his bed grieving his dog. Lennie begs George to tell him again about their future farm. Candy listens in as George lays out their plans, and then he asks George whether he really knows of a place to buy. Although George is suspicious of Candy's intentions, he eventually tells him of a farm they could buy for $600. Candy tells them he has $300 saved in the bank and $50 more coming at the end of the month. He would be happy to add his money to the pool if they would allow him to live with them on the farm. George begins to do the math and guesses that they could buy the farm for $450 at the end of the month. Suddenly George and Lennie's unattainable dream seems within reach.

That night, Curley starts beating up Lennie, but Lennie follows George's orders and allows Curley to punch him. Eventually George cannot stand it and tells Lennie to fight back. Lennie grabs Curley's hand, breaking all of his bones. George warns Curley to tell everyone he got his hand caught in a machine or George will make sure everyone laughs at Curley.

On Saturday night, George goes into town. Lennie joins the black stable hand Crooks in his room and after some conversation, Candy also joins them. Candy tells Crooks about their plan to buy the farm, and Crooks offers to come and work on their land for his keep. The three begin formulating their plan when Curley's wife pops in, looking for Curley. Although Crooks continually asks her to leave, she stays and pieces together that it was really Lennie who broke Curley's hand. They finally convince her to leave by saying they hear Curley coming home. George arrives home and tells Candy and Lennie they should not be in Crooks's room talking to him because he is black. When George reminds them all of the racial divide, Crooks takes back his request to be a part of their farm.

Dreams Lost

On Sunday afternoon, Lennie visits his puppy in the barn, accidentally smacking and killing it when it tries to bite him. When Curley's wife enters, Lennie hides the puppy under some hay. Lennie informs Curley's wife that George has told him not to talk to her. Curley's wife complains about her loneliness and gets Lennie to admit to her that he killed his puppy. Despite Lennie's protests, Curley's wife spills out the story of her missed opportunity. She once had a man tell her she could be in the movies. He was supposed to write to her, but she never received the letter. She married Curley instead.

Lennie opens up and tells her about his love of touching soft things like mice, rabbits, and velvet. Curley's wife invites Lennie to touch her soft hair. As he does, he strokes it harder and harder until she yells at him to stop. Lennie is concerned George will hear and be angry, so he covers her mouth and nose with his hand to make her stop. As she struggles, he shakes her and breaks her neck. Lennie tries to conceal her dead body under the hay and runs away to hide in the clearing, just as George had told him to do if he got in trouble.

Lennie accidentally murders Curley's wife.

Candy finds Curley's wife dead in the barn. He and George discuss what they need to do. They know Curley will want to lynch Lennie for it. They both realize their dream of the nice farm where they will be their own bosses is now gone. When the other men find out what happened, they gather to search for Lennie and kill him. George tells them Lennie would have gone south. George then sneaks off on his own to meet Lennie at the clearing by the pond. Lennie asks George to remind him about the farm, and George recites their dream. He asks Lennie to look at the river and shoots Lennie in the back of the head. Slim tries to comfort George by telling him he did the right thing. Lennie had to be put down, and it was right of George to do it himself.

9

Love as Friendship

The uncommon relationship between two men is the focus of *Of Mice and Men*. George and Lennie could not be more opposite, yet they have been traveling and working companions their entire lives. One way they connect is through the power of their shared dream. Their fellow worker, Candy, and the stable hand, Crooks, both take part in the dream of building a farm together for a short time. But Candy and Crooks are invited in on the plan only after they demonstrate their usefulness in helping George and Lennie's dream become a reality. Finally, the main friendship of the story between George and Lennie must end when Lennie makes the dream impossible. In Steinbeck's *Of Mice and Men*, friendships exist only when self-interest

George and Lennie's relationship at first seems based only on their shared dream of a mutual farm.

Thesis

A thesis is the main argument of an essay. This thesis states: "In Steinbeck's *Of Mice and Men*, friendships exist only when self-interest is involved, but George and Lennie's friendship defies this theme."

Argument One

Argument one states: "George and Lennie seem unlikely friends based on their differences, but they share one common dream." This argument establishes the unusual relationship that is the focus of the novel. It must come first because the other friendships formed in the story are focused around the relationship between George and Lennie and the dream they share.

is involved, but George and Lennie's friendship defies this theme.

George and Lennie seem unlikely friends based on their differences, but they share one common dream. George is a small man who is smart enough to control Lennie through emotional manipulation. On the other hand, Lennie is a large man with a mental impairment. Steinbeck uses a metaphoric language to describe Lennie as animal-like. Lennie "[snorts] water like a horse."[1] He "[drags] his feet . . . the way a bear drags his paws."[2] Steinbeck goes as far as to label him a "terrier who doesn't want to bring a ball back to its master."[3] The strong bond between such unlikely friends is their mutual self-interest. Alone, they would only ever be migrant workers, but together they could buy a farm of their own. Whenever they begin arguing, George recites the common story of their dream, reaffirming the importance of their friendship.

Candy and Crooks become friends with George and Lennie when they can contribute to the dream, but the four are no longer friends when the shared dream is lost. After Candy's dog is put down, he is desperate for friendship. When he overhears George and Lennie discussing their farm dreams, Candy sees an opportunity to cure his loneliness. Although Candy's motivation is companionship, he knows he must show his usefulness to appeal to their self-centered desires. George and Lennie already have each other, so they do not need companionship. Instead, Candy offers them the one thing they do not have: money. Once Candy offers to pay one-half of what

Argument Two

The second argument demonstrates the power of the dream to bring other outsiders into friendship with George and Lennie: "Candy and Crooks become friends with George and Lennie when they can contribute to the dream, but the four are no longer friends when the shared dream is lost." Because it covers two characters, the author uses two paragraphs to support this argument.

it would cost to buy the farm, George immediately welcomes the friendship.

Crooks, the black stable hand, is welcomed into the dream for only a short time. When George is gone for an evening, Lennie and Candy are left without his guidance. They end up making conversation with Crooks, despite the racial boundaries that would normally keep them from associating with him. When they tell Crooks about the farm dream, he offers to do odd jobs around the farm to earn his keep. Crooks sees an end to the isolation he feels as the only black man on the ranch, and Crooks and Lennie are excited to have more help on the farm. The three begin building the dream together until George finds them. He is unwilling to cross racial divides and insists they leave Crooks's room. It is clear George will never allow Crooks to be a part of the plan.

When Lennie kills Curley's wife and destroys their dream, George is forced to put an end to their loving friendship. George knows he cannot save Lennie

Argument Three

The third argument shows that even the main friendship of the story dies with the shared dream: "When Lennie kills Curley's wife and destroys their dream, George is forced to put an end to their loving friendship."

from punishment as he has in the past. Instead, George feels he must kill Lennie instead of watching Curley do it. Although George and Lennie no longer have a mutual self-interest, George gives Lennie this one final act of love and friendship. Right before George shoots Lennie, he recites the familiar words about having their own farm together where they will not have to work for anyone else. Although the dream is dead for George, he keeps it alive for Lennie until he shoots him.

The friendships in *Of Mice and Men* appear to be based on achieving selfish desires. When the desire is within reach, the friendships remain solid. However, when the dream is removed, the friendships also end. George and Lennie are a mismatched couple, but it does not matter because they have a dream that can only be achieved together. Candy becomes friends with them only after he offers to give money toward their future farm. Crooks is welcomed into their circle of friends for only a short time. Crooks envisions receiving their companionship, but he withdraws his desire to join when George makes it clear he will not see past racial barriers. When Lennie ruins the dream for all of them, George and Candy's friendship becomes secondary. In a final act of love and friendship, George keeps the dream alive for

Especially after their clashes in the past, George knows he must kill Lennie before Curley, *center*, does.

Lennie until he shoots him. Lennie dies believing they will still achieve their dream, and George is left to live with the loss of his dream and the loss of his friendships. Although the friendships in *Of Mice and Men* all appear to be based on achieving selfish desires, George's act of love at the end of the novel proves his friendship with Lennie was based on more than only a mutual dream.

Conclusion

The final paragraph is the conclusion. Each argument is reviewed and related to the thesis. The final sentence restates the thesis.

Thinking Critically

Now it's your turn to assess the essay. Consider these questions:

1. What is another argument that could be made to support the author's thesis?
2. One character not discussed is Curley's wife. From the summary chapter, you know she tries to initiate friendship with Lennie by sharing her dream of becoming an actress. What argument could you make to support the thesis of this essay from that part of the story?
3. Do you think it is the shared dream that bonds Lennie and George as the thesis states? For what other reasons do you think these characters could have become friends?

Other Approaches

The love between friends can be just as complicated as romantic love. Friendships can be interpreted many different ways and may even be understood differently by two characters within the story. Another approach to *Of Mice and Men* might apply John Steinbeck's quote, "Try to understand men, if you understand each other you will be kind to each other."[4] A different analysis of the theme of friendship might discuss how loneliness, or the lack of friendship, is the driving motivation for all of the characters in the novel. Friendships are rarely as simple as they appear on first inspection, which means there is always another approach to discover in analyzing this theme.

Feminist Critique of *Of Mice and Men*

John Steinbeck believed understanding others led to kindness. But in *Of Mice and Men*, nobody takes the time to understand Curley's wife. She seems to have no friends. The only one who listens to her is Lennie, and he seems only interested in touching her hair. Also, throughout the entire novel, she is not named; she is only referred to as

"Curley's wife." A thesis for a feminist critique of *Of Mice and Men* might read: Because she is a woman, no one will take the time to understand the motives of Curley's wife, and therefore, she is unable to form any friendships.

Friendship Lacking

The main characters in *Of Mice and Men* are in a battle against loneliness. For example, Lennie's greatest fear is losing his friendship with George, and Curley's wife spends all of her time attempting to find someone who will interact with her and make a connection. An essay analyzing this concept could have a thesis that states: In *Of Mice and Men*, John Steinbeck argues humanity's greatest need is friendship.

Analyze It!

Now that you have examined the theme of love, are you ready to perform your own analysis? You have read that this type of evaluation can help you look at literature in a new way and make you pay attention to certain issues you may not have otherwise recognized. So, why not look for a love theme in one or more of your favorite books?

First, choose the work you want to analyze. Who is the main character? Are there secondary characters? Do characters grow or change through their friendships or love relationships? If you choose to compare the theme in more than one work, what do they have in common? How do they differ? Next, write a specific question about the theme that interests you. Then you can form your thesis, which should provide the answer to that question. Your thesis is the most important part of your analysis and offers an argument about the work, considering the theme, its effect on the characters, or what it says about society or the world. Recall that the thesis statement typically appears at the very end of the introductory paragraph of your essay. It is usually only one sentence long.

After you have written your thesis, find evidence to back it up. Good places to start are in the work itself or in journals or articles that discuss what other people have said about it. You may also want to read about the author or creator's life so you can get a sense of what factors may have affected the creative process. This can be especially useful if you are considering how the theme connects to history or the author's intent.

You should also explore parts of the book that seem to disprove your thesis and create an argument against them. As you do this, you might want to address what others have written about the book. Their quotes may help support your claim.

Before you start analyzing a work, think about the different arguments made in this book. Reflect on how evidence supporting the thesis was presented. Did you find that some of the techniques used to back up the arguments were more convincing than others? Try these methods as you prove your thesis in your own critique.

When you are finished writing your critique, read it over carefully. Is your thesis statement understandable? Do the supporting arguments flow logically, with the topic of each paragraph clearly stated? Can you add any information that would present your readers with a stronger argument in favor of your thesis? Were you able to use quotes from the book, as well as from other critics, to enhance your ideas? Did you see the work in a new light?

Glossary

adapted
When a novel is rewritten for a new format such as a film or a play.

antithesis
The exact opposite.

begrudging
Reluctant.

chasm
A deep hole in the earth.

convention
A commonly used custom.

exposition
A detailed explanation.

initiation
A process of formal acceptance into a community.

lynch
To kill someone illegally as punishment for a crime.

multifaceted
Having many pieces.

naïve
Showing a lack of experience or understanding.

notoriety
Being celebrated or widely known.

passive
Not participating actively.

reiterate
Restate.

servitude
Forced labor.

standardize
To change things so they are consistent with accepted rules.

Characteristics
AND CLASSICS

Love is a common theme in literature. While the theme of love is often depicted as a romantic love, love as friendship is also a common theme of literature, art, and film. Love, which is thought to be essential for the human experience, is usually at least a supporting theme in many works.

This theme often includes:

- A main character who has a romantic love interest
- A highlighted friendship or sibling bond
- A happy, sad, or bittersweet ending
- Challenges or obstacles the lovers must overcome

Some famous works with a love theme are:

- William Shakespeare's *Romeo and Juliet*
- Jane Austen's *Pride and Prejudice*
- Margaret Mitchell's *Gone with the Wind*
- E. B. White's *Charlotte's Web*
- J. K. Rowling's Harry Potter series
- Stephenie Meyer's Twilight series
- Kathryn Stockett's *The Help*
- John Green's *The Fault in Our Stars*

References

Cinderella. By William Peed, Wilfred Jackson, Hamilton S. Luske, et al. Distributed by RKO Radio Pictures, 1949. Film.

Dunton-Downer, Leslie, and Alan Riding. *Essential Shakespeare Handbook*. New York: DK, 2004. Print.

Frozen. Dir. Chris Buck and Jennifer Lee. Disney, 2013. Film.

Hornstein, Lillian Herlands. "Petrarch, Francesco." *The Reader's Companion to World Literature*. New York: New American Library, 1956. Print.

Roth, Veronica. *Divergent*. New York: Katherine Tegen, 2011. Print.

Shakespeare, William, and T. G. Tucker. *The Sonnets of Shakespeare*. Cambridge, 1924. Print.

Sleeping Beauty. Prod. Walt Disney, 1959. Film.

Snow White and the Seven Dwarfs. By Walt Disney, David Hand, Perce Pearce, et al. RKO Radio Pictures, 1937. Film.

Steinbeck, John. *Of Mice and Men*. New York: Penguin, 1993. Print.

Additional RESOURCES

Further Readings

Fry, Stephen. *The Ode Less Travelled: Unlocking the Poet Within*. New York: Gotham, 2006. Print.

Kesselring, Mari. *How to Analyze the Works of William Shakespeare*. Minneapolis, MN: Abdo, 2013. Print.

Sawyer, Jenny. *How to Write an A+ Essay: A Step-by-Step Guide to Acing Your Next Assignment*. Boston: Recap, 2013. Kindle ebook.

Websites

To learn more about Essential Literary Themes, visit **booklinks.abdopublishing.com**. These links are routinely monitored and updated to provide the most current information available.

Places to Visit

National Steinbeck Center
1 Main Street
Salinas, CA 93901
831-796-3833
http://www.steinbeck.org
View a collection of Steinbeck's artifacts, books, and film clips.

The Shakespeare Society of America
7981 Moss Landing Road
Moss Landing, CA 95039
831-633-2989
http://www.shakespearesocietyofamerica.org
Read reviews and view photographs and slides of all things Shakespeare.

Source Notes

Chapter 1. Introduction to Themes in Literature

None.

Chapter 2. An Overview of Disney Fairy Tales

None.

Chapter 3. *Frozen's* Modern Love

None.

Chapter 4. An Overview of Shakespeare's Sonnets

1. Lillian Herlands Hornstein. "Petrarch, Francesco." *The Reader's Companion to World Literature*. New York: New American Library, 1956. Print. 683.
2. Leslie Dunton-Downer, and Alan Riding. *Essential Shakespeare Handbook*. New York: DK, 2004. Print. 457.
3. William Shakespeare and T. G. Tucker. "Sonnet 18." *The Sonnets of Shakespeare*. Cambridge: Cambridge University, 1924. Print.
4. Ibid.

Chapter 5. Shakespeare's Contrasting Techniques

1. William Harmon, C. Hugh Holman, and William Flint Thrall. "Petrarchan Conceit." *A Handbook to Literature*. Upper Saddle River, NJ: Pearson/Prentice Hall, 2006. Print. 378.

Chapter 6. An Overview of *Divergent*

1. Veronica Roth. *Divergent*. New York: Katherine Tegen, 2011. Print. 95.
2. Ibid.
3. Ibid. 101.
4. Ibid. 162.
5. Ibid. 288–289.

Chapter 7. Tris's Self-Love

1. Veronica Roth. *Divergent*. New York: Katherine Tegen, 2011. Print. 30.
2. Ibid. 12.
3. Ibid. 47.
4. Ibid. 87.
5. Ibid. 176.
6. Ibid. 311.
7. Ibid. 315.
8. Ibid. 200–201.
9. Ibid. 209.
10. Ibid. 487.

Chapter 8. An Overview of *Of Mice and Men*

1. Susan Shillinglaw. "Introduction." John Steinbeck. *Of Mice and Men*. New York: Penguin, 1993. Print. xxiv.
2. Ibid. xxv–xxvi.
3. John Steinbeck. *Of Mice and Men*. New York: Penguin, 1993. Print. 4.
4. Ibid.
5. Ibid. 26.

Chapter 9. Love as Friendship

1. John Steinbeck. *Of Mice and Men*. New York: Penguin, 1993. Print. 4.
2. Ibid.
3. Ibid. 10.
4. Susan Shillinglaw. "Introduction." John Steinbeck. *Of Mice and Men*. New York: Penguin, 1993. Print. ix.

Index

About the Author

Maggie Combs is a freelance writer. Her principal area of interest is literary education. Maggie lives in Minnesota with her husband and three active sons. She enjoys relaxing at her cabin, reading novels, and studying interior design.